Let the Feline Fun Begin!

ROCKWELLHOUSE

© Rockwell House Ltd
First Published in UK in 2007 by
Rockwell House Ltd
www.rockwellhouse.com

Text by Elissa Wolfson
Illustrations by Stephanie Piro
Design by James Deighton Graphics

ISBN 978-1-906060-01-5

Printed in UK

Dedication

To my parents, George and Doris, and my brothers,
Ira and David, who took in and loved our childhood cats.

To the wonderful members of the Cat Writers
Association for generously sharing ideas and support.

To my husband Steve, who accepted cats into his life as part
of a package deal, and became a loving cat dad.

101
Cool Games
for
Cool Cats

Mind-bending Games
To Play With Your Cat

Elissa Wolfson
with illustrations by
Stephanie Piro

What's in it for Me?

CONTENTS

101 Cool Games

Why Cats (and You) Need to Play

Watch any two kittens go about their day. These hyperactive, insane little fuzzballs will leap with glee upon anything that flutters, scoots, or dangles—including each other. It doesn't take long to realise that the act of playing is hard-wired into the feline species. But today, with cat owners working long hours, teenagers away at college, and kids off at soccer practice or the shops, many cats are left to their own devices for extended periods of time. "Latchkey kitties" is a phrase invented by pet behaviourist Warren Eckstein to describe cats left alone in the house all day.

What happens when cats can't satisfy their innate need to play? Veterinarian Ilana Reisner is director of the Behaviour Clinic at the University of Pennsylvania. "We don't really have a way to measure depression in cats," she says. "But we do know that they sometimes behave in depressed ways." Such behaviours may include lethargy, lack of grooming, excessive sleeping, loss or gain of appetite and weight, aggression, and destructive behaviour. The latter may be the beginning of a downward spiral, where a displeased owner becomes even less likely to play with his or her cat, and the cat

"If you suspect your kitty may currently be lonely or under-stimulated, you may be right."

becomes even more bored and destructive as a result. Once the cat-owner bond begins to dissolve, the outcome is not likely to be a happy one.

Contrast this to a cat-owner who provides "preventative stimulation"—an enriched environment and quality playtime each day. Can this be you? If you are willing, the rewards are great. Enlivening your pet's indoor life will result in a contented, healthier, and better behaved cat—and lower veterinary and cat therapy bills for you. But perhaps the greatest reward is the deep bond that will develop between you and your cat, and the enjoyment you'll find in each other's company.

If you suspect your kitty may currently be lonely or under-stimulated, you may be right. The antidote is spending high-quality time together every day. This will goes a long way toward providing these sensitive, intelligent creatures with the stimulation and variety they need to be physically and mentally healthy. And where behaviour problems already exist, enriching your cat's environment is an important part of the solution.

Start putting a little sparkle into your cat's life. Try a new, healthy brand of cat food.

Hide food treats around the house. If you have a piano, see if your feline maestro enjoys making her own music by walking on the keys. Share a bit of your scrambled eggs. Finally, consider adopting another kitty—even if your pre-existing cat complains at first, like any creature, she will eventually appreciate one of her own kind to speak cat with.

Mix it up a little! The cat games listed in this book will give you how-to's on dozens of activities, including taking your leashed kitty for a walk outside, popping on a kitty video, growing your own catnip, and buying or making exciting cat toys. But most important, it will give you a multitude of ideas for playing with your cat—an essential activity which provides bonding and exercise opportunities. This in turn keeps your cat's weight under control, and helps develop muscle tone, agility, and stamina. And regular play helps guard against your cat's most dangerous enemy: boredom. As an additional perk, you get exercise too!

Caring for your cat is good. But having an amazing interactive relationship is so much better. An abundance of affection, grooming, and daily play sessions will get your furry pal purring again. She will in turn be there to cheer you up when you need it!

DANGERS

Inside Cat or Outside Cat?

Why not simply let your cat play outdoors where she can get all the exercise she wants? For one thing, it's a dangerous world out there. Nothing in your cat's evolutionary history has prepared her to deal with zooming cars and busy streets. Rabies, fleas, ticks, big dogs, toxic antifreeze, pesticides, cat fights, inhumane humans, and especially cars, all have the potential to make your veterinary bills go up and your cat's life expectancy go down.

As well, outdoor cats take a heavy toll on wildlife. Free-roaming cats kill songbirds at feeders, fledglings that cannot fly, and small rodents — a critical food source for owls and hawks. As songbird populations decline, our appreciation for them has grown. Birding enthusiasts number in the millions. A fair number of "twitchers" also own cats. Because they love both their cats and the wild birds, they are in a dilemma when it comes to letting their cats outdoors. But by enriching their indoor environments, we can keep our cats happy, while also keeping the wild birds alive.

As responsible pet owners, it's up to us to provide our cats with healthy, happy, secure lives. To do the cat population and the local fauna both a favour, spay or neuter your cats, and support efforts by local cat protection groups to trap, neuter, and return feral cats in order to bring their populations down. Then keep those predatory pussycats inside, where they—and the wildlife—are safer.

"Nothing in your cat's evolutionary history has prepared her to deal with zooming cars and busy streets."

Kitty Enclosures: A Cathedral of Fun

Not so long ago there were only two choices for cat-owning households: confining cats to the house, or letting them roam freely. Indoor cats can live happy lives, particularly if they have been kept inside since kittenhood, and especially if their thoughtful owners provide a stimulating environment of toys, catnip, places to climb, scratching posts, and lots of attention. But indoor cats do require some extra house cleaning, and often, some extra reupholstery. And, particularly if you are one of the many kind-hearted humans who have given a home to a former stray or feral, come springtime, you may find yourself with a kitty who wants to slip outdoors at every opportunity.

If your cat is as desperate to go out as you are to have her stay in, the two of you may be able to compromise on an outdoor enclosure. Such enclosures allow your cat to experience the joys of the great outdoors—without the hazards. You can make your outdoor enclosure even more appealing by furnishing it with tree limbs and stumps, ladders, tyres, hanging toys, and boxes for your cat to curl up or hide in. Tarpaulins can provide shade and protection from the rain. Enclosures can range from the simple to the sublime.

The enclosure built by Joan and Don Blackburn leans toward the sublime. These cat heroes had their 19 cats in mind when they designed their home in 1989. "We looked at our backyard and thought, 'Wouldn't it be great to create a kind of outdoor tree house for the cats?'" recalls Joan Blackburn. The Blackburns' builder proceeded to design the 8ft x 10ft structure with holes cut into the roof so that the four oak trees inside could protrude out of the top.

Inside were ledges of varying heights for sunning and perching. The trees inside served as huge scratching posts. A screen door allowed the humans in, and a tunnel linked the enclosure to the house. There a cat door allowed the cats to enter as they pleased—which they did, practically year-round.

"They loved it!" says Joan. "Many of our cats were foster cats or rescued strays, and the enclosure helped them transition into pet-hood." From the safety of their outdoor sanctuary, her cats monitored the dogs and squirrels outside, perched on the ledges, slept in the sun, ran up and down the trees, and made short work of any moth or grasshopper that made the fatal error of wandering into their realm.

At one point, the Blackburns had 26 cats. "I was so glad we built the enclosure," says Joan. "It enabled us to take them all in." For anyone considering a similar structure, the Blackburns have a word of advice: trees grow. After a decade, the oaks' expanding girth started pushing the boards apart. Today the Blackburn's eight cats content themselves with a screened-in porch. "We're known around town as 'the cat people,'" laughs Joan. "I'm sure that's how we'll be remembered. But the cats pay us back many times over with their presence."

"For anyone considering a similar structure, the Blackburns have a word of advice: trees grow."

To Buy or to Fabricate?

To build a basic outdoor kitty enclosure, you'll need to attach six-foot-high wire fencing to metal or wooden fence posts of equal height, pounded well into the ground. Remember that cats can jump up to five times their own height! Unless you're adding a roof, bend the top two feet of fence at least 45 degrees inward.

For those without the time or tools to construct one, pre-made kitty enclosure kits are available online.

All Mine!

"Enclosures allow your cat to experience the joys of the great outdoors — without the hazards."

Catnip: Favourite Feline Perfume

Fortunately, one item beloved by cats everywhere is non-addictive and perfectly safe: catnip. Although not all cats are affected, most adult cats love to roll in, rub, and even eat the stuff. The chemical within catnip, called nepetalactone, triggers this response. After several minutes of generally going nuts, the cat acclimates and loses interest. Two hours later, the cat may "reset" and respond again. Some cats may become over-stimulated to the point of aggressive play; others may simply become relaxed. Kittens under six months old seem to be immune. Apparently, catnip works on big cats like lions and tigers too!

Growing catnip is easy, as the plant tolerates a variety of conditions. Buy some seeds or small plants at your local nursery. Grow it outside, as the indoor plants may be pruned by your over-zealous kitty each time they rear their tiny green heads! Any sunny location, either in the ground, or in a pot on your balcony will do. Wait until the plant has grown a dozen or so leaves, then pinch or snip off the topmost leaves. Do this regularly to prevent the plant from flowering, and to encourage bushy leaf growth. In the autumn, well before the first frost, strip the leaves from the stems and store them immediately in an airtight plastic or glass container in the freezer—enough to get kitty through the winter.

Catnip Lift: A Perennial Pick-me-up

When you sense your cats need a lift, remove a handful of catnip leaves from the freezer, let them warm up to room temperature for a few minutes, and toss them to your grateful kitties. Fresh catnip leaves can be crushed a bit to release the scent, then sprinkled on the carpet or, for easier cleanup, on a large cardboard box top or on a towel placed on the floor. An occasional catnip spree is perfect for chasing away the new kitten blues!

Catnip-filled soft toys are fun to bite, kick, and carry around. To use the leaves for stuffing toys, first dry them out: tie a bunch at the base with some yarn and hang it upside down anywhere with good air circulation. A month or so later, strip off the dry leaves and flowers, and store them in a glass jar till needed. Since the plant is a perennial, it'll be back the next spring, and all the following ones too—much to your cat's delight!

"An occasional catnip spree is perfect for chasing away the new kitten blues!"

Kitty Catering: Working for their Food

Your cat's ancestors had to catch 10 or 20 insects, birds, mice, and other small creatures daily to survive. They spent hours foraging each day. Compare this to today's pet cat who gets a days' worth of food all in one big glob, without having to work for it at all. Mimicking a more normal feeding behaviour will provide your cat with physical exercise and mental stimulation, and help prevent the boredom and obesity associated with abnormal feeding patterns—such as leaving out a full food bowl at all times.

Feed your cats at least twice daily; there should be no leftovers. Also, devise ways to regularly allow cats to hunt for their food. I used to feed both of my cats just before blithely leaving the house for work each morning. One day I noticed Fuzzball was getting a bit tubby, and soon discovered that she was polishing off her morning meal much faster than Stretch. Upon finishing, she would worm her way into Stretch's food bowl and get herself a double portion!

I now monitor meals, and have taken to feeding Stretch on top of the refrigerator—too high for fat Fuzzball to jump. There Stretch can eat her meal at her leisure, undisturbed, in her usual dainty fashion. Meanwhile, Fuzzball is working for her food—chasing it around the house, or solving food puzzles.

Another cat owner deals with a similar situation by feeding her thinner cat inside a closet with a sliding door, that she sets open just enough to exclude Mr. Fat Cat from his food-stealing ways.

Food can also be used as a reward for performing tricks and obeying verbal directions.

When teaching my cats to use a scratching post, I tucked cat biscuits or treats between the sisal ropes, so they'd have to get into "scratching" position to get at the morsel. And because I want them to have good associations with their carrying cases for the times we need it, I regularly leave the cases open with — you guessed it— kitty treats inside!

"... a more normal feeding behaviour will provide your cat with physical exercise and mental stimulation, and help prevent boredom and obesity ..."

Persuasion: Tricks and Treats

Yes, cats can be trained, even to do tricks! Encouraging and rewarding positive behaviour are the best ways to do so. Never use physical or verbal abuse. Where possible, just ignore or redirect undesired behaviour. For example, if kitty starts to scratch furniture, redirect her back to the scratching post and reward her when she uses it. Cats can be taught to sit when asked, jump through a hoop, lift a paw, jump up on surfaces when invited, and come when called, using food treats, praise, strokes, catnip, and toys as rewards. Rewards can also be used to train a cat to do even more useful "tricks", such as allowing teeth brushing, nail trimming, and grooming.

"Always give rewards immediately and consistently during the learning process."

The best time to teach a cat to do tricks is when the cat is slightly hungry, the house is quiet, and you are both in a peaceful mood. To teach your cat to sit, hold a treat in front of her nose and then move it upward. As the cat's head goes upward, the haunches should go down. If not, very lightly press down on the hindquarters with your other hand. Say "sit" as the cat sits and give her the treat at the same time. Praise the cat lavishly upon completion of the task. Always give rewards immediately and consistently during the learning process. Repeat the task several times a day until your cat "gets it", Once the desired behaviour is learned, give rewards intermittently.

When rewarding your cat, choose treats that are made of high quality ingredients (read those labels!), moderate to low in calories, and appealing to your cat.

Many cats enjoy the attention and stimulation associated with training. Being trained can be helpful and even lifesaving under certain circumstances. For example, "sitting" and receiving a treat at the veterinarian's office may distract and calm an anxious cat; coming when called can help recover a lost kitty.

Start with things your cat already likes to do. Using a feather toy on a wand as a target and praising your cat when she follows it, you can teach her to climb up a cat

"The best time to teach a cat to do tricks is when the cat is slightly hungry, the house is quiet, and you are both in a peaceful mood."

Climb!

post, jump to a nearby chair, down to the floor, up onto the sofa, across the top of the sofa, down to the floor, and then repeat. Your cat can learn simple words like "jump", and "down." This sort of agility route can provide much-needed exercise. "If learning is fun, play can be used to achieve far more than distraction," says cat author Barbara Florio Graham. "I made training techniques fun, persuading my cat Simon Teakettle not to fear or dread his collar and leash by treating them initially as toys. I've continued with this over all of his 18 years, teaching him a new behaviour every year. Many of these are things I wanted him to learn for safety reasons and/or my convenience, such as sit, stay, come, or get down. I use toys as well as treats to reward him for these 'tricks.'"

Kitty Flicks: Movies for Cats!

If your cats are like most, they rarely watch TV. Can they actually perceive what's on the screen? Indeed, they can—but often choose not to. *The Simpsons*, *Survivor*, even *Sex in the City* all get four paws down. Cats simply don't find people shows interesting.

But cat movies are different. You can spice up your cat's life with DVDs like *"Reality TV for Cats,"* which lasts for almost two hours and can be set to run continuously. Such DVDs provide indoor kitties with vicarious outdoor pleasures, such as birds flocking at feeders, masses of mice, darting aquarium fish, squirrels cracking nuts, crawling insects, and more.

These DVDs can be used as a special treat, or to keep your cat entertained when you're away. Bill Hayward, creator of the kitty video *"Feathers for Felines,"* notes: "Some veterinarians and cat owners use our videos to help their cats get through illnesses, and as part of their recuperation process."

Field Test: A Furry Focus Group

When testing kitty DVDs, the advantages of a multi-cat panel became clear. Our two cats' reactions varied wildly. If my cat video reviews were based solely upon Stretch's response, I would have declared them all a hoax! We did everything short of rubbing catnip on the TV screen, but our restless three-year-old tabby always had better things to do than watch videos.

However, our year-old calico, Fuzzball, quickly became mesmerised by the tantalising creatures inches from her nose, literally rising to the occasion now and then on her hind legs, the better to bat at the on-screen birds and squirrels. Other cats reportedly crouch, stalk, and pounce. But Fuzzball was mostly content to sit, eyes darting and ears twitching, making darned sure no critter got off the screen under her watch.

Kitty videos make great gifts, not only for your own favourite feline, but for friends with cats as well. A veritable smorgasbord of kitty delights awaits!

Create Your Own Kitty Couch Potato

- Place your cat about three feet from the TV, with the screen at eye level. If your TV is high off the floor, place a stool or chair at "pawing" distance.

- Minimise the number of people present, turn off radios, and darken the room.

- Draw your cat's attention by tapping the TV screen lightly, but don't make a fuss about the video or try to force your cat to watch it.

"...Fuzzball was mostly content to sit, eyes darting and ears twitching, making darned sure no critter got off the screen under her watch."

Toys for Kitty: Accessory or Necessity?

Toys are absolutely necessary for your cat's well-being: they serve as an antidote to boredom and an outlet for cats' instinctive prey-chasing behaviours. As an added bonus, humans often have as much fun with cat toys as their kitties do! Studies show that cats play best and most often with interactive toys—that is, when you, the favourite human, are moving the toy around while your cat leaps, swipes, and chases. Then, playtime doubles as "people time" and becomes a bonding experience for you and your cat. Whatever type of play your cat prefers, it's all the more engaging when you are engaged in it too.

> *"... aluminum foil, plastic ballpoint pen caps, old baby rattles, paper bags, crumpled cellophane, drinking straws, old socks, ribbons, and twisty ties can all have a new life."*

Before you spend lots of money on cat toys, take a look around your house. You may be surprised at how many of the common household items you already have are favoured by cats. Safe, simple cat toys can be created from many of these things. It's a great way to recycle! Things like used aluminum foil, plastic ballpoint pen caps, old baby rattles, paper bags, crumpled cellophane, drinking straws, old socks, ribbons, and twisty ties can all have a new life. Plus, putting those wine bottle corks to good use is a great excuse to invite friends over for a glass of wine!!

No matter which toys kitty loves best, she'll love them even better if you rotate them regularly. New or rotated toys hold cats' curiosity and interest for longer periods of time. Store them in a closet or drawer and bring them out again a week later—they'll seem brand-new, and you'll be providing a fresh, intellectually stimulating environment. To entice your cat to play with a new toy, rub it with catnip leaves—or try some spray-on catnip, available at pet stores or online. Keep a variety of toys on hand—a big, soft one to wrestle with, a small one to bat around, and a dangly one to leap at. Remember that real prey doesn't run toward a cat—it runs in the other direction! So, to stimulate the chase response, toss balls and other toys away from, rather than toward your cat.

"Often, the things most attractive to cats are the things that are most dangerous."

Playing Safe: Cat-proof Toys

Though the imagination of some cats is boundless when it comes to inventing games with household objects, you will need to set some boundaries. Often, the things most attractive to cats are the things that are most dangerous. Loose string, yarn, thin rubber bands, and Christmas tree tinsel can all become tangled in your cat's intestines if swallowed. Soft wood can splinter. Plastic bags can suffocate a small cat, or cause intestinal blockages if pieces are torn off and swallowed. Bead, buttons, marbles, tiny SuperBalls, and other small round items are choking hazards. Avoid or "cat-proof" any questionable toys by removing plastic "eyes," and other small parts that could be chewed off and ingested. Cat-proof your home by hiding string, ribbons, yarn, rubber bands, paper clips, pins, needles, thumb tacks, dental floss, and the like.

Use caution with any toy that has attached string or yarn, as kitty could become entangled, or swallow and choke on it, with potentially fatal results. To make these toys safer, run the strings through narrow plastic tubing, and make sure

"Lots of toys are available online, but unless you are already familiar with the toy, it's always nice to handle it first ... "

the strings are attached to something on either end; for example, a stick on one end and a cork on the other. Or, simply remove dangling toys altogether when you're not there to supervise.

Commercial Toys: Choosing and Perusing

Depending on the age and disposition of your cat, many of the toys you bring home from the store may get the furry cold shoulder. Many shop-bought catnip-filled creatures are simply too heavy—or the catnip may have been on the shelf too long and lost its pizzazz. Lots of toys are available online, but unless you are already familiar with the toy, it's always nice to handle it first, the better to decide whether it's worth buying.

Favourite purchased toys include catnip mice, standard-sized SuperBalls, fishing pole-type toys, realistic-looking toy fish that wiggle and bob in sealed bowls, plastic balls with bells inside, and sisal-wrapped toys. Most cats love interactive toys that a person manipulates to entice the cat to play. There include toys attached directly to the end of wands, as well as toys attached to strings which are attached to wands.

"The better you know your cat, the better you will be at choosing the right games."

Playing with Purpose: How and When to Play

To round off a perfect relationship, make time for fun and games. How much time? Play for an hour a day with a kitten, broken up into four 15-minute sessions daily. Ten minutes twice a day for a teenage cat and as little as five minutes twice a day for an adult cat could make all the difference between a bored overweight "cat potato", and a healthy, happy, and affectionate kitty. But make sure the games stay fun for everyone: Never encourage young kittens to attack your fingers or toes. "Remember that what is cute in an eight-week-old kitten will not be cute in an eight-month-old cat!" notes veterinarian Wayne Hunthausen, a cat behaviour consultant. Think how betrayed your adult cat will feel when she is scolded for performing the same antics that used to delight her favourite human. Instead, teach her early on that human body parts are not toys. "When your kitten gets that look in his eye, you can help ward off impending ankle attacks by tossing him a toy that you just happen to have in your pocket!" says Hunthausen. "Feathers dangling from toy fishing poles, catnip mice, foil balls, ping pong balls, or even walnuts are all great fun for your kitten to chase."

To get your cat to get up and go, use interactive toys that you can keep jiggling. If the toy stops moving, your cat may consider it successfully "killed", and lose interest. Put these special toys away at the end of each play session to prevent her from becoming bored with them; she will then eventually associate these fun toys with you. Most cats love fishing pole-type toys with feathers or stuffed toys tied to the end of the string. Once your cat gets going, you may witness astounding leaps, twists, and other death-defying feline acrobatics! Other cats prefer the thrill of the chase. For these cats, toss a standard-sized SuperBall or foil ball down the stairs, up the stairs, across the floor, even into the tub. Activities like these, spelled out in detail in the chapters that follow, will help your cat find her inner hunter!

Not all cats enjoy all games equally. And most cats aren't at their most playful upon awaking from a nap, or when they're focused on their next meal. The better you know your cat, the better you will be at choosing the right games. Take your cat's age and disposition into account. Most kittens are insatiable when it comes to playing, and will play with almost anything, anytime, anywhere.

"Once your cat gets going, you may witness astounding leaps, twists, and other death-defying feline acrobatics!"

But many healthy adult cats enjoy playing throughout their lives. Even senior cats may turn kittenish when attacking a catnip mouse or chasing a feather lure on a fishing pole. Older cats may prefer a few select activities. Curmudgeonly cats may only want to play when they are in the mood. Shy cats may be easily outplayed by bolder cats; you may need to conduct separate play sessions with each cat. Sometimes your cat will initiate a play session, by reaching for your pencil as you're writing, or leaping at your shoelace as you're removing your shoes, or just rolling over on her back and giving you that certain look. Your cat is sure to inspire many games during your life together. The games described below are a great way, literally, to get the ball rolling!

The Lowly Cardboard Box

It's the bane of every cat owner's existence: you spend lots of money on the latest in robotic mice, only to have kitty demonstrate much more interest in the box her expensive new toy came home in! Think of all the money you can save from now on. Even large unglamorous cardboard boxes make for enjoyable cat games. Consider these uses: Turn the box over so the open side is at the bottom. Cut a small hole in the edge and put a catnip mouse inside. Watch kitty try to grab the mouse. Scrunch up a few pieces of paper and throw them into an open cardboard box, especially one just a tiny bit too small for your cat to fit into. Watch the fun.

Boxy Basketball

2

Ask your local supermarket or off-licence for a large, clean cardboard box with a lid. If it has holes in the sides, all the better! Crumple up paper balls in a variety of textures and sizes from office paper, catalogues, junk mail, or paper bags, and heap them into the box lid. Find yourself a comfortable sofa or armchair and, setting the box a few feet away, settle down with the lid of paper balls, and proceed to toss them into the nearby box one by one. Kitty will literally have a ball intercepting them from either inside or outside the box. When all the balls have been tossed into the box, invert it onto the lid and begin again.

3 Budget Kitty Condo

Take those lowly cardboard boxes a step further—create a kitty condo! Place two large, strong boxes side by side on the floor and cut a hole into the adjoining wall of each box, so kitty can pass from one to the other. Then cut another hole in the top of one, and place another, smaller box on top of that hole, open side down. Anchor the flaps of the boxes resting on the floor with bricks or large, flat stones, and duct tape the boxes together for greater stability.

Budget Scratching Post

Wise owners know that scratching is a normal, healthy cat behaviour. Recycle an old carpet, or ask your local carpet shop owner to save you some carpet remnants that would otherwise get thrown away. Cut long rectangular pieces of carpet, about as wide and tall as your cat is when stretched out full-length. For an average cat, that's about two and a half feet long, and five inches wide. There are dozens of ways to use these. Cats often prefer a variety of scratching surfaces and positions. They use different muscles in scratching vertical surfaces as opposed to horizontal. For vertical scratching, glue or nail the carpet remnant securely to an out-of-the-way wall. For horizontal scratching, glue or nail it to the floor. To train your cat to use a scratching post, reward with treats and praise. Also put catnip, treats, and toys on or near the post. Wherever you fasten it, be sure it is very stable; kitty will come to distrust a wobbly scratching surface, and move on—possibly to your sofa. Many cats prefer the "wrong side" of the carpet to the fluffy side for scratching purposes. Yours might rather just scratch a cardboard box or an old phone book.

Experiment till you find the texture and orientation your cat loves best!

Luxury Kitty Condo

5

Cat owner Shara Rendell-Smock reports, "My sweet babies enjoy their wooden, carpet-covered kitty condo, with three levels; the top has a hole to jump through to sit on that level. It's about six feet tall and looks so tatty. I bought it for £3 at a car boot sale about 30 years ago and have since moved it with me wherever I go."

'Au Naturel' Scratching Post

6

Some cats have fond genetic memories of their jungle cat days. Bring them home a log or tree stump, and let them take a walk on the wild side. A stump that's about a foot across and three feet tall can be used as both a scratching post, and a napping perch. If you're getting it directly from the woods, let it dry out thoroughly in the sun, and let all the insects escape before you bring it into the house. Set it down on a newspaper in a place where kitty likes to scratch. She may even prefer it to the couch.

What's brown, cheap, crinkly, recyclable, and loved by cats everywhere? Simple paper grocery bags! If it's a shopping bag, first remove any handles so as not to entangle your cat. (Plastic bags are *not* a good idea, as many cats like to chew and ingest the plastic). A large paper grocery bag lying on its side is great fun for a cat to pounce out of and dash back into. And if you have two cats, they'll have a great time hiding and ambushing one another from their bag "caves." Cut some holes in the bottom of the bag for added interest. To make it interactive, scratch softly on the outside when she's inside. Then quickly switch to the opposite side—watch the fun. A fun variation: Attract cat with toy, toss toy in bag, and watch bag explode as cat dives inside!

What's in the Bag?

Whatever kitty likes best! An extra-small plain brown bag becomes even more exciting with a few noisy goodies inside. Blow inside the bag like you would a balloon, to puff it out a bit before filling. Try various combinations of cellophane, walnut shells, aluminum foil, and crumpled pieces of other plain brown bags, and of course, a big spoonful of dried catnip. Twist and then close off the top of the bag with a twisty tie, plastic rubbish bag tie, or a fat rubber band, such as the kind that holds broccoli stalks. Toss the bag to your cat, or leave it in a secret hiding place for her to find when you go off to work.

9 Bagging the Cat

Put a kitty treat at the bottom of a long, thin, wine bottle bag, set it on the floor, and watch her try to wriggle her way in. When kitty finally gets to the treat, both of you can re-treat — that is, she can wriggle back out, and you can toss in a second treat. If she breaks the bag, no worries—it transforms easily into an alternate cat toy by crumpling it up into a tight round ball.

Bag Tunnel

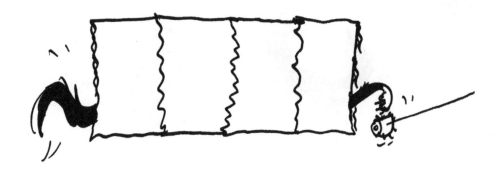

Cut the bottoms off of two or three paper grocery bags, and then tuck them partway inside one another to create a paper bag tunnel for kitty to crawl through. Pull a toy on a string through the tunnel for her to chase down. Dangle the toy, first at one end of the tunnel, then at the other end. Watch her double back and do a ferret imitation.

Tiny Bubbles!

An inexpensive—or free—bottle of bubbles can provide hours of fun. You can create your own bubble mix with one-half cup of water and two tablespoons of non-toxic, unscented washing-up liquid. For a unique twist, try catnip-scented bubbles made with water that has been steeped overnight in catnip and strained. Using the store-bought wand or a homemade one made from wire bent into a circle (the larger the circle, the larger the bubble), dip the wand into the liquid, and with your mouth close to the circle, blow gently and slowly until you get a sizeable bubble! Gently flick the bubble off the wand and blow it over to your waiting kitty, who will either try to catch it, follow it around, or simply watch it float by, obviously enchanted.

Now take that bottle of bubbles, or any small plastic water bottle half filled with water, cap it tightly, and spin it around. Kitty will enjoy watching and hearing the water slosh around, and she may even lend a helping paw. When the bottle stops and points to kitty, obviously, it's time to give her a kiss!

13 Fizzy Fits

Pour some carbonated water into a shallow dish. Some cats will enjoy watching the fizzing bubbles and maybe even taking an occasional swipe at them.

Have a bunch of small pillows at hand near your own pillow. Wait till kitty is at the foot of the bed, then toss pillows gently in her direction and see if she enjoys intercepting them. For more stalwart cats, try tossing over a regular human-sized pillow. However, avoid playing such rough-and-tumble games with cats that are either shy and fearful, or older and arthritic.

15 Mice in the Blankets!

With you under the covers and kitty on top, wiggle your fingers or toes until she pounces. Immediately withdraw the fingers or toes and begin wiggling them elsewhere on the bed. When an opportune moment presents itself, toss the blankets over her and roll her up inside them.

Under-Cover Kitty

Lift up the front end of your covers and see if kitty enjoys worming her way under the blankets, then burrowing her way through to the light at the end of her self-made tunnel. For an added challenge, tuck in the covers all around and see if she can still find her way out.

17 Peek-a-Boo

While kitty is still under-cover, scratch or poke the covers from above on the opposite end of the bed and watch her scoot after the "intruder" from below. Scratch or tickle kitty herself while she's under the covers. Surprise her by flinging back the covers to expose her unexpectedly, and then quickly cover her up again. Peek-a-boo!

Climb Every Mountain

While you're under a thick blanket or quilt, make a kitty mountain by raising your knees. Begin by setting your cat on top of your knees and let her hang out there awhile, playing "queen of the mountain", and surveying her domain. Then surprise her by slowly collapsing your knees to one side, giving her a gentle tumble. Raise your knees up again and she may clamber right back up the mountain, eagerly awaiting the next quake!

Note: This game may not be suitable for senior cats.

19 Billowing Blankies!

Stand on top of or at the side of the bed, with kitty on the floor. Raise and then slowly lower the entire sheet at once, making it billow as it descends. Watch kitty attack the billows and make them disappear. For added fun, billow another sheet down on top of her.

No matter what's under the rug, if it moves, kitty will love it — to pieces, that is. Lift the corner of a rug, and toss a toy on a fishing pole string underneath it. Tug on the string while kitty watches, to make the rug-rat move. Any self-respecting cat, no matter how old or blasé, will be compelled to dive at it from above, eventually working her paws, and perhaps her whole body underneath the rug—whatever it takes to get that creature out of there!

21 Pulling the Rug Out

Wait till kitty's sitting on a convenient throw rug, and then slowly and gently begin pulling it out from under her. Watch her slide and scamper as she tries to figure out what's going on. She may retaliate by staging a mock attack on the fickle rug just to show it who's the boss. This works with sheets as well!

Shine a torch or lamp on a white wall in a darkened room, and make some shadow puppet creatures for kitty to leap at.

See the Light!

23

Darken a room with a bare wall. Turn on your laser pointer and beam the red light onto the wall. Taking care not to shine the beam into your cat's eyes, slowly, slowly, slowly inch the beam forward, then inch it back, then speed it up, zigzag it across the wall. Kitty will "light up" as she follows and leaps up at the beam. When she "attacks", quickly move the beam elsewhere.

Hmmm, that doesn't smell like a mouse, but it sure is fun! Watch her climb the walls, leaping as high as she can to get at the mysterious glowing "creature".

You! A great variation on "peek-a-boo" is to peek at your cat out of a slightly opened bathroom door. Enhance the excitement by running an old cotton glove slowly up and down the edge of the door. When kitty leaps up at the glove, withdraw it quickly and close the door a bit further. Wait a few seconds, then peek out, and poke the glove out again. Watch kitty attack and retreat just a few feet away, attempting in her catty way to lure you out from behind that door!

Door Scrunchies

door
stop

Prop an inside door most of the way open with a doorstop. The door should open out to make about a 30° angle with the wall behind it. Get your cat to sit in this space and poke one of your stockpiled cotton gloves, small sock rolls, or hair scrunchies into the narrow slot between the middle and top door hinges. Run the scrunchy slowly up and down the length of this slot. Kitty will leap at it from the other side of the door, and every once in a while, she'll surprise you by grabbing it and pulling it right on through to "her" side of the door! Continue till you run out of gloves, socks, and scrunchies—then you can raid her pile for the next round.

26

Spread the newspaper out across your knees. Of course, you know better than to plan on actually reading it! Watch kitty jump up onto the newspaper, onto the exact article that you would have read if you could have, then turn the page on her. Then another, and another. See if she enjoys reading upside down in her newspaper tunnel.

Newspaper Scruffle

Paul Glassner, cat owner and editor at the San Francisco SPCA, invented this new game—along with a new word. "I like to lay full sheets of newspaper on the floor, then subtly (SUBTLY!) move something (not your own hand!) beneath the paper. Use something long, like a ruler, or the wand of a cat toy. The sound and sight are irresistible. The cat will scruffle (there's the new word) among, and tear up the paper, making for a wonderful, delightfully noisy play session."

The newspaper fun's not over yet! "With one hand, lift up a sheet of the newspaper by one corner," suggests Paul Glassner. "With the other hand, show the cat his/her favourite toy mouse. Let go of the newspaper and as it floats to the ground, toss the mouse underneath. A guaranteed pupil-popper — the cat will pounce in, on, under, and through the paper!"

Stairway to Heaven

If you have an appropriate staircase in your house, this will provide an excellent aerobic workout for you both! Place kitty near the top of the staircase. Stand at the bottom and toss a paper, rubber, or foil ball against the wall, near where the cat is sitting. Or stand at the top of the steps with your cat and push the ball gently down the first few steps. She'll likely go right after it, batting it about till it reaches the bottom. Fling it against the wall again. Repeat until exhaustion sets in.

Fluttering Strips

Rip up a newspaper into long thin strips. Using masking tape, attach the strips to your banister, about two inches apart, and all up and down your staircase. The strips should almost, but not quite, reach the stairs. Turn a small fan on low, and aim it at the strips. Watch kitty have a blast tearing them all down.

31 Cat Wheelies

Take advantage of your cat's seemingly innate love for suitcases! Leave out a partially opened small wheeling suitcase—preferably lined with something soft. When she's lying inside, tilt the bag up ever so slightly and slowly begin to pull her around the house. Experiment with different floor surfaces. Carpeting provides the smoothest ride, doorjambs the bumpiest. Put a few folds into a large rug for a roller coaster effect. She may leap out—or she may love it!

A non-wheeled variation of the above. Poke a hole in the centre of a sturdy shoebox near the top of one of the short sides; thread through it a four foot length of thick string or nylon line. Knot one end of the string to prevent it from passing through the hole in the box. Allow the cat to investigate the contraption, then, using the string, pull the shoebox around the house as kitty watches. If she doesn't get the idea to jump in, lure her into the box with a few kitty treats and very slowly begin to pull her around the house. Stand in an open area and circle the box around yourself a few times for a merry-go-round effect. Try figure eights or hairpin turns for more adventurous kitties.

Exploring New Places

Give your cat a change of scenery now and then. As interesting as your house is, especially after all your loving improvements, it will never be quite as interesting as a place she's never seen before. Particularly if your cat is young, and/or confident and sociable, consider teaching her to walk outdoors with a harness and leash—then take her with you to visit friends and relatives.

Saddle Up

PARK

Make the harness into a game, starting with having her wear it for just a few minutes at a time around the house, all the while lavishing kitty with praise and strokes, treats, and scratches behind the ears. Work your way up to longer periods of time. When she's comfortable with the harness, clip on the leash and let her go wherever her little heart desires. When she gets the hang of that, encourage her to go where you want her to go, using the gentlest of tugs, followed by an immediate release. Go slowly and patiently and praise kitty to the high heavens for every step in the right direction. Graduate to walking around outside your house in a quiet, dog-free yard or park.

35 Kitty Gyms

Inside of every house cat is the memory of a wild cat ancestor who spent lots of time in the trees. From a cat's point of view, vertical space is a highly desirable commodity which increases the overall space available to them, and gives them the opportunity to survey their domain. Provide cat trees, preferably with hiding spots, cat perches, and shelves. If you're one of those rarified cat owners who will go all out for their cats, consider buying and installing a ramp and shelf system that allows kitty to climb up to just below ceiling level, and then proceed to walk around some well-placed catwalks. Be sure to provide some lookout spots from which to view the top of her favourite human's head.

If your cat enjoys the company of other cats or dogs, set up a play date with some of her furry fitness buddies. Unless the pets involved have a history of living together, it's best not to leave them completely unsupervised. But if everyone seems to be getting along, owners can relax, have dinner or watch a film while their pet pals chase each other around the house.

Tag, You're It!

Cat owner Janet Blizard says: "My cat Squeaker likes to initiate a vigorous game of tag—under rules that seem to make allowances for the fact that I have limited mobility."

"Squeaker 'tags' me and runs, and then waits patiently until I limp almost close enough to touch her. Then she bolts again. When she decides she's had enough, she lets me tag her to end the game."

Laundry Basket Boxing 38

This game works best with two cats and one lightweight plastic laundry basket with holes. Turn the basket upside down with kitty number one underneath. See if kitty number two takes advantage of his "outside" status by sneaking a few jabs into the holes at his caged sibling. Kitty number one may retaliate by boxing right back. If you have only one cat, poke a feather into one hole, then another on the opposite side, then back to the first side—you get the picture! When the basket is right side up—preferably full of warm-from-the-dryer clothes—most cats adore jumping in for a nap.

High Rider

Many cats enjoy getting a human's eye view of the world from the vantage point of their favourite person's shoulders. Initially, set her on your shoulder for just a few minutes at a time. Wrap a towel around your neck and the tops of your shoulders to prevent accidental clawing. Some cats like the drape-around-the-neck position, while others prefer the peek-out-over-the-shoulder technique. Bolder kitties may enjoy the making-like-a-parrot style of perching directly atop the shoulder. Whenever you sense your cat is comfortable, try rising slowly from a chair while holding her securely onto your shoulder with one hand. Walk around the house slowly, letting her see and sniff all those interesting things that are usually out of reach. For a special treat, stow some kitty treats on the shelf-tops you pass along the way.

Tunnel Vision

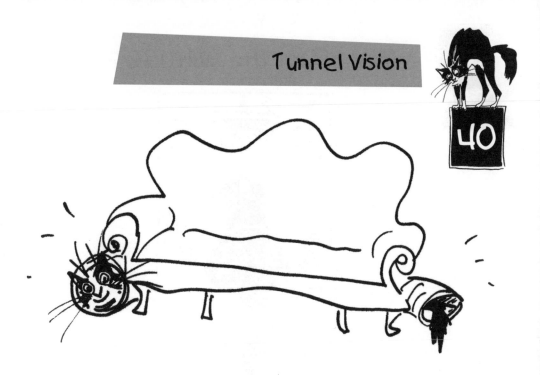

Visit your local plumbing store and purchase a length of lightweight, flexible tubing at least six feet long, and six and a half inches in diameter—depending, of course, on the size of your house, and the diameter of your cat! Run the tubing behind your sofa, going in at one end, and coming out at the other. Toss a few balls, catnip mice, or treats inside and watch kitty use the tunnel as part of her motorway system—or adopt it as her personal hidey-hole.

41 What's Out the Window?

Stoop way down to cat's-eye level, and check out the scenery outside your windows. From a cat's point of view, nothing is more boring than pavement. Lawn is just a small step up from being a kitty desert. A tree or shrub is much better. Hang a well-stocked birdfeeder just on the other side of the window and set out a comfy perch—such as a window seat or kitty condo—to view it from. Bird feeders and window perches give cats the feeling of being outdoors without the risks. Kitty heaven!

This and That

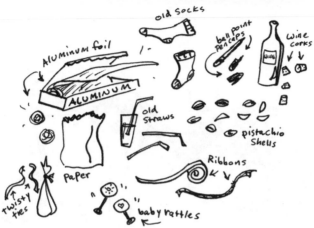

old socks

Aluminum foil

ball point pen caps

Wine corks

ALUMINUM

old straws

pistachio shells

paper

Ribbons

twisty ties

baby rattles

Your cat can help you with this one. Pay attention to the things around the house that attract her, and between the two of you, you can devise some games and toys from them. A few "home-made" toys to try: Fly a paper airplane over kitty's head. Wide rubber bands can be sling-shot across the floor so kitty can give chase—but avoid thin, ingestible rubber bands. Foam shoulder pads from an old blouse or dress make excellent "mice" (try rubbing or spraying catnip on them). Round plastic shower curtain rings will shower your cat with fun, either when linked together and hung in an enticing spot to bat around, or as a single ring to hide or carry about. Plastic bottle caps, package bows, and anything else that's fun to carry or bat around can all be test-tossed across the room. If they're still there in the same place the next day, discard them and try something else.

Toy Central

Put a few safe kitty toys (no strings or ribbons please) in a pretty basket and set it on the floor where it can jazz up an otherwise barren corner of your house. Rotate the toys in the basket at least once a week. Now your cat can help himself to a toy anytime he feels like playing, even when you're not around!

Have a Ball

44

Roll a piece of paper into a nice tight ball and swat it lightly across a bare floor. Voila, you've created the simplest of all cat toys, and used it for the simplest of all cat games! Most cats respond by attacking the ball where it lands, at which point they will either swat it back, or wait for you to toss it again. Sturdy paper—the noisier, the better—works better than newspaper, so feel free to recycle those brown paper bags, and your least favourite bills. Experiment to find a ball of the size and weight your cat loves best. She may love them enough to take and hide them everywhere. You may find them all over the house!

Have a Super Ball!

45

If you have a standard-sized rubber SuperBall handy, great—if you don't, go buy some! The SuperBall's light weight, sky-high bounces, and completely unpredictable trajectories make them irresistible to cats of all stripes (or no stripes!). Plus they are great for tub or sink soccer. Other cats are entertained by tennis balls. Kitty may enjoy lying on her side with a tennis ball between her front paws and kicking at the ball with her hind feet.

Blow up a giant plastic lightweight beach ball and begin getting kitty used to it by just setting it in a corner for a few days. Then gently roll the ball toward her, or give it a tap with your foot and see if she bats it back. In a large open area, work your way up to lightly kicking the ball in the general direction of your cat, and take turns intercepting each other.

Foiled Again!

47

Got any semi-clean, gently-used aluminum foil lying around? Here's yet another recycling opportunity. Take a piece measuring roughly 9" by 12" (remember it's not rocket science!). Crumple it up till you can't squeeze it any tighter, and shape it by rolling it between your palm and the kitchen counter, until you have a tight, round ball. Toss it away from your cat and watch her and the ball both take off. Much as they love paper balls, most cats love foil balls even more because of their light weight and delicious skittering sound. For a bit of variety, scoot the ball around an empty bathtub, which now becomes a playpen!

Place kitty in the centre of your dry bathtub and roll a standard-sized SuperBall over the edge and down into the tub. A captive ball is much more fun than one that escapes under the sofa. Kitty and the ball will both be bouncing off the tub walls before long. Your job is to keep the ball rolling, preferably around and around the perimeter of the tub. For extra fun, add another ball into the mix. Ping-Pong balls and plastic practice golf balls with holes work well for this game too. You'll probably want to remove the balls from the bathtub before bedtime, or you may lose some sleep— two o'clock in the morning seems to be a prime time for this game.

49 Sink Soccer

If your cats are like mine, they're up on the edge of the bathroom sink at the slightest opportunity, ready for anything from swatting your trouser drawstrings to critiquing your mascara application technique. It's a good opportunity to involve kitty in a game of sink soccer. See "Tub Soccer"— similar rules apply. Roll a ball around a dry bathroom sink and see if she dives in!

Floatable Boatables

Fill the sink or tub with water and, with kitty on the edge of the sink or tub, flick a few floatables across the surface. Ping-pong balls, corks, especially floating cat biscuits may prove too fascinating to resist reaching in a paw and batting it around, or in the case of the cat biscuit, extracting and eating it! For added appeal, drip the tap very slowly and see if kitty enjoys catching those drops too.

51 Sock It To Me!

Take an old ankle-length sock of yours; smaller children's socks work even better. Starting with the toes, fill 'er up with two heaping tablespoons of your own home-grown, previously dried catnip. Add a tablespoon of empty pistachio shells or a tablespoon of large dried beans, and top it off with the crinkly crumpled cellophane from your latest CD or potato chip bag. This combination is sure to induce clutch-n-kicks and other forms of temporary kitty insanity! As with any stuffed toy you make, be careful not to over-stuff the sock. Feel and listen to the toy before it's finished—the stuffing should swish around and make the appropriate kitty-attracting sounds, and the toy should be light enough for kitty to pick up in her mouth and fling around. When you and kitty are both satisfied, tie off or sew up the open end and sock it to her! Take an old pair of socks—preferably thick ones, and preferably ones you don't

want to wear ever again! Stuff one inside the other as if you were pairing them up for your dresser drawer, then throw in a spoonful of catnip for good measure. Toss the sock ball across the floor, and see if kitty attacks it. She may proceed to roll onto her back with her new prey clutched in her front paws, biting at it from the front, and kicking at it from the rear. That sock ball doesn't stand a chance!

LeotardTug-o-War

Cat lovers make up that small minority of women who don't mind finding a large run in their stockings. We simply look at the ruined hosiery and think of all the new cat toys we can now make! The very simplest stocking toy to make is the tug-o-war "rope". Just cut off the leg. That's it! Dangle the toe end in front of kitty's nose. When she grabs on, pull back. You pull, she pulls, you pull...you get the picture. At the appropriate time, depending on your mood, you can either let go suddenly, and give her a tumble—or pretend she's overpowered you and let it slip reluctantly from your fingers. Watch her scoot away in victory, with her hard-won prize trailing behind her!

Leotard Dangle

Similar to other danglers, only much bouncier and stretchier! Take the leftover stocking leg and cut that one off too. Drop a whole pecan or walnut down into the toe area to provide a bit of ballast. Dangle the toe a few feet above kitty's head and watch her jump for joy.

55   Leg Worm

If you don't happen to have a small daughter on hand, pop over to your local clothes shop for some small children's leotards or leggings. Cut off one leg about a foot up from the toe. Spoon in a pinch of catnip, a few pistachio shells, more catnip, some small empty snail shells, more catnip, a bit of crinkly cellophane, more catnip—just keep going till your worm is just full enough (but not too full!). Tie off or sew up the open end, and watch your creation worm its way into your kitty's heart.

Save those wine corks! They transform easily into mice. Rub or spray catnip onto a cork, then take a knitting needle or skewer, and poke a hole through the cork lengthwise. Run a length of embroidery thread or sturdy string through that hole, making a knot at both ends and leaving enough sticking out of the rear end to make a nice long mouse tail. If you string the cork mouse up by its tail to a longer ribbon, you can dangle it overhead for kitty to jump at, or drag it along the floor to provoke a mock-attack. Meanwhile, you can drink the wine that the cork came out of, which makes it even more fun...

57 Cork Fishing

Using scissors or a skewer, poke a hole through the length of a wine bottle cork, and thread a sturdy six-foot length of string through it. Knot the string on one end to keep it from passing through the cork. Tie the other end securely to a short stick. Using the stick as your "fishing pole" and the cork as kitty bait, go fishing! Drag the cork across the floor, over the furniture, and around the corner, and let the cat stalk and pounce on it. Dangle it a few feet above your cat, and let her leap at it. See what you catch!

Solo Fishing

See "Cork Fishing" activity. Using the same toy, set the string to an appropriate length by winding it around the "fishing pole", then secure the stick to the refrigerator door handle, wedge it into a drawer or between sofa cushions, or set it on the counter with some very heavy objects on top of it. Kitty can amuse herself by swatting the cork while you read or watch TV.

Jingle Jingle
Jingle Jingle
Jingle

Save those empty thread bobbins. Run about a foot of embroidery thread, nylon thread, or sturdy string through two small matching bobbins placed end-to-end. Make a large knot on either end of your creation to hold it in place. For added fun and more sound effects, tie on two small bells, one on each side. Roll it past kitty's nose and see if she reaches out a paw to help it along. To make it more interactive, tie a long ribbon onto the string between the two bobbins so you can roll this mini-two-wheeler along from a standing position. Pull slowly at first, then speed up. Keep varying the speed, and see if you can entice her to leap on it. Let kitty rock and roll to her heart's content!

Bobbin on a Wire

60

Position a three-foot length of sturdy elastic string, or an old guitar string catty-corner across an unused corner of your house. Run the string through the centre of a medium-sized bobbin with several feathers glued onto it, then attach it to both walls with two small eyelet hooks—one threaded directly into each wall—about four feet from the floor. Loop the string through the eyelets and tie it off so it is fairly taut. The triple action of the bobbin as it spins around, bounces up and down, and scoots side to side will entertain kitty immensely.

Empty cardboard tubes from toilet paper rolls make fun rolling toys. They become even more fun if you "unwind" a bit of the cardboard first. This gives kitty a foothold into the tube, which will then spiral away as she rolls, bites, and tears into it.

Shreddy Confetti

Take an empty cardboard toilet paper tube, and stuff it with toilet paper.
Watch kitty have a blast pulling it all out and turning it into kitty confetti.
Join the fun by tossing the confetti into the air all around her.

Autumn Leaves

This game was invented by Fuzzball who watched intently as I did my annual low-budget interior decorating—lightly gluing bright red, yellow, and orange autumn leaves onto a hallway wall. The idea was to keep a bit of autumn colour around all year long—maximum beauty for a minimum price. But Fuzzball had other ideas. She soon figured out that her reward for a leap up the wall was a crunchy leaf fluttering to the ground, which could then be attacked and shredded. Great fun for kitty—so long as you use non-toxic glue, and don't mind skid marks on your wall!

Maple Twirlers

Find a nearby maple or "sycamore" tree and collect a dozen or so of its twirly seed pods in the late summer and early autumn. The tree's idea is to have its young whirl away to sunny, fertile ground where they will have a better chance of growing up. Your cat's idea is that suddenly a dozen little green spinning helicopters have flown into her home, for her personal leaping and catching pleasure.

All-Natural Hockey Pucks

flick

Tuck the tip of your forefinger into the centre of your thumb and practice mastering the art of making a sharp sudden flick of your forefinger by pushing off from the thumb. This is the best way, bar none, to send a "hockey puck" flying across the floor. Once you've mastered the finger flick, find yourself a puck. Ice cubes and grapes are popular choices. If you prefer something a little less messy, try flicking a walnut, or a small dry pine cone. Whatever puck you choose, it should be either too large to swallow, or harmless if ingested. Then, proceed to send that puck skittering it across a smooth floor, with kitty in hot pursuit!

If you have a long feather handy, lightly run it along the length of your cat till she feels compelled to grab it. Tickle her from one side, then the other as she wiggles to catch the tickly feather. Then hold the feather up high and drop it. See if she can intercept it before it hits the ground.

67 Gone Fishing

Snip a pom-pom from the top of an old hat or sock. Rub catnip all over it. Thread an eight foot length of sturdy string or ribbon through it, knotting it off on one end. Tie the other end securely to a slender wooden or fibre-glass stick about three feet long. The stick serves as the "fishing pole". Cast the "mouse" casually past your cat, and then withdraw it, slowly at first, then quickly and erratically, imitating a confused rodent as best you can. Once kitty pounces, tug at the mouse to pull it away, then scoot it quickly to the opposite corner of the room.

Stick three or four fluffy feathers into the cut out bottom of a Styrofoam cup. Poke a hole into the centre of the cup bottom and thread through it a three-foot length of sturdy elastic thread, with a knot on one end to hold it in place. Get the good china out of harm's way! Make the feathers "fly" through the air, up, down, and in circles around kitty's head. Allow the "birdie" to land briefly, and then take off again. Fly it up and down the stairs for even more exercise.

69 Gone Mousing

Take a sturdy shoebox and cut small mouse hole-shaped arches into all four sides. Open the top and drop in several homemade or store-bought catnip "mice" into the centre of the box. Close the lid and set the box in front of the cat. Enjoy her efforts to liberate the mice from their "cage". When she has succeeded, drop the mice back in again.

Set your cat on a table. Take a foil ball and send it skittering over the edge of the table. See if she grabs it before it goes over. If not, wait till she jumps down to chase it, and then toss it back up onto the table. Put the ball right at the edge and see if she bats it over. If she goes down after it, toss it back up again. Kitty aerobics, anyone?

Hide and Seek

"Found" toys are often much more attractive than a toy which is obviously introduced. If you've just purchased or made a new toy for kitty—say a catnip sock—refrain from tossing it right to her. Instead, put it under a blanket near where she likes to nap, behind the sofa, or tucked between an armchair seat cushion and the back of the chair. Let her experience the joy of discovery.

For a "hide and seek" variation, show your cat a favourite toy and let her watch as you hide it under a blanket. If she seems puzzled about what to do next, jiggle the toy under the blanket to encourage her to "find" it.

Kitty Sachet

If you're handy with a needle and thread, take some old fabric scraps and cut them into three-inch squares. Using sturdy thread—embroidery thread works particularly well—sew two squares together around three sides to form a small pocket. Fill the pocket with noisy, crunchy objects. Throw in a small jingle bell for added effect. Don't over-stuff—and don't forget the catnip! Sew up the last edge, and hand it over. Kitty will have fun attacking and flinging her sachet bag around the house. As with other small cat toys, they can end up in some pretty interesting places.

Bat the Bow Tie

Cut a narrow strip of thin cardboard about an inch wide by eight inches long. Sturdy fabric, like denim, or a strip of plasticised paper works even better— also a great way to recycle those temporary wristbands from music festivals. Give the strip a few twists at mid-point until it takes on the appearance of a bow tie. Tie a ribbon or old shoe lace around the twisted middle part, and dangle it in front of kitty's nose so she can bat at it, or high above her head so she can jump at it. Hang it from a curtain rod or doorknob, so she can amuse herself while you supervise.

75 Draw Straws

Plastic drinking straws are easy to find, safe, inexpensive, and great for teething kittens. But cats of all ages love straws for their chewability and crunchy sound. "Pet" the cat with the straw, or brush it across kitty's front paws, or drag it across the floor to initiate some interactive play, holding on to one end while the cat bats at or chews the other end. Or tie a knot in it and let kitty chase his plastic prey. Animal shelter volunteer Sharon Melnyk comments, "Straws are an approved cat toy at our local shelter. They can be tossed away rather than disinfected—a big plus among staff. When we work to socialise and modify the behaviour of play-biters and scratchers, straws are a good tool to keep feline teeth and claws at a distance."

Pipe Cleaner Insects

Bend a pipe cleaner into a circle and twist the ends together. Then twist the middle of the circle a few times till you have a figure 8—or with a bit of imagination, a butterfly. Bend the "wings" together slightly so the creature isn't totally flat, and "fly" it over your kitty. Or, twist a pipe cleaner around your finger to form a curlicue, then toss it past your cat to bat around or carry about in her mouth, as she sees fit. Fit three pipe cleaner circles inside each other to form a ball and roll it past your cat. Try other shapes and see which she likes best.

77 Boxing Glove

Take an old gardening glove, or a thick, oversized winter or leather work glove.
Onto each finger, sew or securely tie a lightweight dangly toy on a ribbon or string.
Vary the lengths of string, and vary the four or five toys themselves.
One can be a cork, one can be a pipe cleaner butterfly, one can be a cardboard bow
tie, etc. Slip the glove on your hand and wiggle your newly embellished fingers!

Screw an eyehole into the ceiling above an empty area suitable for play. Thread a long piece of ribbon through it, then tie the ribbon on one end to the eyehole, and on the other end, to the top hook of a wire coat hanger. Bend the hanger hook into a loop so the ribbon can't slide free. Tie three safe toys—such as a cork, a catnip mouse, and a pom-pom, along the bottom part of the hanger—with two of equal weight at the ends and one in the middle—using shorter pieces of ribbon threaded through plastic tubing for safety. Tape down the ribbons holding the toys to the hanger, to prevent them from sliding along the hanger and tangling up. The toys should dangle about two feet above kitty's head. Watch her bat at one toy, and set the whole contraption in motion!

Old Fashioned Fetch

Some cats will fetch everything and others won't fetch anything—ever!
Still others can be, if not exactly taught, encouraged to do so. See if there's
anything—a paper ball, a plastic milk jug ring, a catnip toy, etc.—that your cat
particularly enjoys carrying about in her mouth. If so, toss it across the room
and if she picks it up, meet her wherever she's carried it, praise her
extravagantly, and toss it again. Slowly increase the distance between yourself
and kitty and call to her as she's carrying the object. Eventually she may get
the idea to bring it to you. Or not...

High Jump Hijinks

Find your cat's favourite lightweight toy—such as a cardboard bow tie, cork, or pom-pom. Secure it to a length of string on a fishing pole and dangle it about two feet above her head. If she seems reluctant to leap for it, glue some feathers on, and then jiggle the toy to make it even more enticing. When she finally springs, see if you can beat her to the punch by snatching the toy enticingly just beyond paws' reach. Raise the bar a foot higher next time around, and then yet another foot higher. Surprisingly, most healthy cats are capable of jumping over five feet high from a sitting position! Every so often—and always as a grand finale—let kitty make her catch and "win" the game.

"I hold on to a scarf and shake it at cat's eye level or a bit higher," reports cat owner and writer Anne Leighton. "This works especially well with a withdrawn or chubby cat. They grab and hold on to one end of the scarf. Then I put my hand in the middle and let the other end drop and dance a bit. The cat will usually let go of the end he's holding, and reach for the new one. Sometimes I use two scarves for a few cats but I'm not the best multi-tasker!"

Curtains for Kitty

I had sheer drapes covering an ugly brick wall in a former apartment and my cats took to climbing up them. Those drapes moved with me to every new apartment, and now I use them to make tents on our collapsible wooden drying rack. The cats will sit for hours among these drapes!

Cat Biscuit Chase

"Feed kitty her dry food piece by piece," suggests cat owner and writer Beth Adelman. "Toss the biscuit and let her chase after it, as she would chase prey. To ensure that kitty gets plenty of exercise, toss each piece down a long hallway, up onto the couch, across the room, or up the stairs. It sounds time-consuming, but isn't—you can feed them their evening meal in about five minutes."

Ping Pong Din-Din

"Feed kitty her dry food in a big bowl, then fill the bowl with ping-pong balls.
Now kitty has to dig through and push out the balls to get to the food,"
recommends Beth Adelman.

Treat Balls

Treat balls are a sort of food puzzle—commercially available little hollow plastic balls that twist apart so you can put food inside, with a cat-biscuit-sized hole in the centre. Kitty has to roll the ball around the room to make the food slowly drop out. When introducing the device, bat it around for her until she gets the idea.

Food in a Tube

Save those toilet paper and paper towel tubes! Cut out small holes, just slightly larger than the type of cat biscuits your cat eats, at random points in the tube. Demonstrate to kitty how rolling the tube will dispense the food, and let her take over from there. For an added challenge, tape paper over one or both ends of the tube to seal off these food-escape routes.

Cut a hole just big enough for a curious paw or two into the lid of a sturdy shoebox. Fill the shoebox with crumpled balls of paper and aluminum foil, walnuts, cornstarch packing pellets, and some cat biscuits—then replace the lid. Watch kitty go fishing! See if she succeeds in pawing the food out.

Here a Treat, There a Treat

If you feed your cat canned food spoon by spoonful, you can do it all over the house to get kitty moving around. One spoonful on top of the cat tree, one on the couch, one under the dining room table, one on the windowsill, etc.

89 Treasure Hunt

Hide dry cat food around the house, in different creative places—such as behind the sofa, inside the kitty condo or carrying case, under a blanket, and up and down a staircase. Let your cats go "hunting".

Set three plastic cups upside down on a table or floor. Invite your cat over and let her watch while you put a kitty treat under one of the cups. Shuffle the cups around a bit. See if she picks the correct cup to knock over!

91   Food on a Frisbee

Another way to exercise your feline chow-hound is to spread a spoonful of canned food onto a lightweight plastic yogurt or Tupperware container lid. Set the lid down onto an uncarpeted floor. Kitty's licking action will slide the lid forward and she will get some exercise as she follows her food across the floor—at least until she learns to lick it into the nearest corner! If you don't quite have the heart to make kitty work so hard, you can simply flatten the canned food against the side of her usual ceramic bowl to at least slow her down a bit.

Any plushy stuffed toy you buy for your cat should be just as safe as one you'd buy for a toddler. Machine washable is a nice plus too, considering the toys' inevitable rendezvous with the backside of your fridge! Stuffed animals are good for several purposes. Some cats love to wrestle with their stuffed animals, in which case the creature should be somewhat sizeable. Legs and a tail make these beasties even more enticing. Or your cat may have a favourite soft toy that she enjoys cuddling or sleeping with. If so, don't rotate that one—leave it out for her all the time. Other cats may enjoy carrying about a tiny stuffed creature. "My cat plays on her own with small, lightweight fabric mice," says cat owner Sharon Melnyk. "She prefers the knitted/crocheted variety. I've seen her toss the mice in the air and bat at them along the floor, and I've found them buried among the sheets and blankets of my bed."

93   Twisty Ties

Fuzzball loves the little twist ties that come on bread wrappers. She even puts them in her water bowl, leaves them there, then gets them out later and plays with them again. Maybe she thinks that's a safe place to keep them. She plays with these for hours on end—despite her box full of shop-bought toys!

Brush Me!

94

Whenever Stretch sees her brush, she just falls at our feet for a good solid half-hour of brushing.

Pony Tales

Our friend's male cat loves to get into her daughter's room and steal her ponytail holders. They find them all over the house.

Bottle Caps

Our foster cat loves plastic bottle caps. If I want him to come, I get one from my stash and tap it on the countertop. Poof! There he is. He carries it around in his mouth from place to place, then knocks it around on the floor until it disappears under the refrigerator. I think he likes the way it bounces so unpredictably.

97 Take a Bow

Fuzzball loves bows (the pre-made kind). The shinier, the better. She plays fetch with them, chases them around the house, and tosses them in the air. By far they are her favourite toys. Stretch's favorite game is to tear through the house with Fuzzball. She periodically pauses, then jumps up, and hugs a doorframe on her way back down.

Our cats, like most, adore sitting in an open suitcase—preferably when we're trying to pack it.

Any sort of hidey-hole will do, such as a blanket or towel draped over the arm
and back of the couch—but they won't get into their cat condo!

Animal Magnetism

Fuzzball has developed a passion for pulling the magnetic letters off the fridge and playing with them on the floor. Problem is, she keeps bopping them under the freezer and losing them. One day I noticed there were hardly any letters on the fridge. So I got a stick and a torch and poked around under there, and half the alphabet came out. She was so pleased to get them back.

We were in stitches!

Post-Chase Lounge

After all that playing, kitty needs a nap! All other things being equal, she'd much rather nap in a warm, sunny spot. Notice all the household hot spots that your little sun-worshipper uses throughout the day, and then make little kitty nests for her in these same spots. Enhance her favourite windowsill—which is probably too narrow to get in a really good nap—by installing two brackets on either side of the window, and laying a foot-wide shelf across the brackets at the same level as the windowsill.

And Finally...

...the Greatest Cat Toy of All

Of all the cat toys out there, there is only one that is simultaneously soft and warm, chases and pursues, dispenses treats, and squeaks rewardingly when pounced upon. Cat lover Darlene Arden sums it up best:
"Her very favourite cat toy...is me."

Hiss Hiss
scratch
CLAW
SPIT
HISS
GROWWL

FIZZY
WATER

=